NOAH

Retold by Susan Dickinson
Illustrated by Sally Holmes

CARNIVAL

Once there was a man called Noah. Noah worked hard. He and his three sons toiled in the fields from morning to night.

But most people didn't like work.
They preferred to have a good time.
And when God saw this he was not
very pleased.

One day, God spoke to Noah. He told him to build a boat, or an ark, big enough to house himself and all his family. It must also be big enough to take two of every kind of creature that walked or flew.

The next morning Noah and his
family set out to cut down trees to
start building the ark.

First they laid down the keel. Then they built curved ribs for the sides. Then they walled the sides with planks of wood, leaving small openings for windows.

While they were working, other
people came to see what they were
doing. "Why are you wasting your
time with that thing?" they said
scornfully. "Come and enjoy
yourselves." Noah and his family
were too busy to reply.

At last the ark was finished. Then God spoke to Noah again. He told him that there would be a great flood which would cover the whole Earth. But because God was pleased with Noah, he and his family would be safe. They must go into the ark, taking with them a male and a female of every creature.

Over the next few weeks, Noah and
his sons searched the hills and valleys

for two of every creature they could
find, and led them to the ark, to safety.

Finally, Noah and all his family went in. Noah pulled up the great door and shut it fast. And then it began to rain.

It rained and rained and rained, for forty days and forty nights, without stopping. Noah looked through a window in the ark and he saw that they were afloat on a vast sea of water. Nothing else was to be seen.

For one hundred and fifty days the ark floated on the sea. Then, slowly, the waters began to go down. Still the ark floated on. Suddenly it stopped. It had hit a mountain top. What should they do now?

Noah decided to release a bird
through a window. The first bird he
chose was a raven. But after the
raven had flown over the ark once, it
disappeared and they never saw it
again.

Seven days later Noah decided to
release another bird. This time he
chose a dove. In the evening the
dove came back and it was carrying
a little branch from an olive tree in
its beak.
Seven days later Noah released the
dove again. This time it did not
come back.

Then God told Noah that he could come out of the ark, bringing all his family and all the animals with him. Noah and his sons let down the great door so that it made a bridge and out came all the creatures that had spent so many days in the ark.

Noah and his family were delighted
to be on dry land once more. They
knelt down and touched the earth
and said thank you to God for
bringing them safely through the
flood. Suddenly in the sky there was
a rainbow, stretching right across
the Heavens.

And God said to Noah. "This is a sign of my promise to you. Whenever you see a rainbow you will be reminded that I promise never again to send a flood to destroy the beautiful Earth I have given you. Look after the Earth. Take care of it, so that your children and your children's children may grow up to enjoy it."

Carnival
An imprint of the Children's Division
of the Collins Publishing Group
8 Grafton Street, London W1X 3LA

Published by Carnival 1988

Text © 1986 William Collins Sons & Co. Ltd.
Illustrations © 1986 Sally Holmes

ISBN 0 00 1944 66 5

Printed in Great Britain by
PURNELL BOOK PRODUCTION LIMITED
A MEMBER OF BPCC plc